S0-BXV-073

The Morning After Mourning

Joy Comes in the Morning

The Morning After Mourning

Joy Comes in the Morning

VICKEE MARTIN, RN, BSN

Pleasant Word
A Division of WINEPRESS PUBLISHING

© 2003 by Vickee Martin, RN, BSN. All rights reserved.

Printed in the United States of America

Packaged by Pleasant Word, a division of WinePress Publishing, PO Box 428, Enumclaw, WA 98022. The views expressed or implied in this work do not necessarily reflect those of Pleasant Word, a division of WinePress Publishing. Ultimate design, content, and editorial accuracy of this work are the responsibilities of the author.

No part of this publication may be reproduced, stored in a retrieval system, or transmitted in any way by any means—electronic, mechanical, photocopy, recording, or otherwise—without the prior permission of the copyright holder, except as provided by USA copyright law.

All scripture references are taken from the King James Version of the Bible.

ISBN 1-57921-580-7
Library of Congress Catalog Card Number: 2003100189

To my sons Christopher Martin and Jerome Martin, who have always stood by me. To my daughter-in-law Angela Martin, who I feel privileged to call 'daughter'. To Patricia Wolfe, Beverlee McGowan, Janie Ewers, and Dana Sindt, each of whom I feel blessed to call 'friend'.

Contents

Introduction

Sorrow affects us all, and during our lives we grieve on many occasions. The death of a loved one, a divorce, or loss of a job can affect us profoundly and will cause us to grieve.

Grief is hard work. The more devastating a loss is to you, the more your grief will need work, and the harder you will need to grieve. Knowing the tasks and stages of grief will enable you to work through your grief.

The Lord is the only one who understands your grief completely, and He can provide the best source of support. Jesus said, 'Come unto me, all ye that labor and are heavy laden, and I will give you rest' (Matthew 11:28).

Finding a willing friend or family member to listen and help you through your grief will also help you with your grief work. Remember, the very worst grief is your own, but effective grief work cannot be done alone.

Grief

In my distress I cried unto the LORD, and He heard me.

Psalm 120:1

Your son's daughter moved out of state to attend college. On her way home for the holidays, she was killed in an auto accident.

Your daughter calls home weeping. Her husband has asked for a divorce.

Your wife was diagnosed with a terminal illness and was told that she had two months to live. Only two days later, she experienced extreme pain, and an hour after being admitted to the hospital, she died. Your ten-and twelve-year-old sons aren't telling you how they feel, but they fight much of the time and are constantly acting out at school.

Your husband just returned to work after a long recovery from an illness, only to be told that fifty per cent of the employees would be laid off. He has only three years' seniority.

How will you cope with any of these losses? How will you help your son, daughter, spouse, or yourself? What will you do?

What will you say?

Sorrow is the proper reaction to a severe loss, and it needs to be released. It is important to let sorrow flow.

Grief is defined as keen mental suffering over affliction or loss. Grief is a process—a period of time in which you seek to come to terms emotionally with loss.

The grief process begins with your initial awareness of your loss and is probably the most

painful emotion that you will ever experience.
Recovery from loss will be easier if you:

1. UNDERSTAND the stages of grief.
2. BELIEVE that you will adjust.
3. LEARN TO ACCEPT your loss and grow from your experience.
4. SEEK HELP when you need it.

Betty's Story

My soul is also sore vexed: but thou, O LORD,
how long?

Psalm 6:3

Joe and Betty had been married for thirty-
seven years. They lived in Denver, Colorado and
had four children; one son and three daughters.
Joe was a good provider for his wife and children and was willing to help in the home. He
taught business management, Spanish, and music. Betty worked as a nurse.

All four of Betty and Joe's children received
college degrees, married, became parents, and
were working in their chosen professions.

Joe loved his grandchildren and was active in their lives. He took the time to listen to their needs and desires. Their school functions were important to him, and he encouraged and helped them in their studies.

Joe and Betty were diligent workers in their church. Joe was a music director for many years, while Betty was a pianist. Together they prepared many activities and programs for special holidays and occasions, for both Sunday School and church.

Joe had been chronically ill for thirteen years. Though his physical condition had been declining, he wanted to go to Portland, Oregon, for their church camp meeting. They were in Portland seven days when he became quite ill with peritonitis. He was too sick to return home for treatment. In fact, he was admitted to the intensive care unit at a Northwest hospital.

As they sat in the hospital emergency room in Portland, Betty felt a tightness in her throat. Her chest felt heavy, as if her heart would break. She had a hollow feeling in her stomach. Her two friends offered her something to eat and drink, but even out of politeness, she could not accept. 'You need it for strength,' they told her.

'No, I just couldn't,' she answered, feeling a sense of confusion. She felt restless. It was difficult to concentrate on what the doctors were saying to her. She couldn't think of the answers to the questions they kept firing at her. 'Oh. Joe's doctor's name in Denver is . . .' Her mind went blank. 'Yes, I know the information you need to know is critical for treatment.' As she began to search through her purse, she stated, 'I do have his name and twenty-four hour number, somewhere.'

After four weeks in ICU and two major surgeries, Joe succumbed to his long illness. Three of their four children came to town to see their father for the last time.

The last song that Joe sang in the hospital before he died was, 'Hold On.' To Betty, the message was, 'Never give up, but hold on to God's unchanging hand.'

Joe's death left Betty with a sense of numbness. She had difficulty sleeping. When she finally did get to sleep, she woke up early. Joe had always been her friend and prayer partner and had been there when she needed him. He was an attentive listener, and now when she desperately needed his support, he was gone. Sometimes she felt his presence or heard his voice. That was a comfort to her, even though she felt sad and lonely.

Betty ran from her grief for almost two years. For several months after Joe's death, she visited her children who lived out of town. She went to Israel for three weeks, to Oklahoma for a family reunion, to Oregon for a church camp meeting, and on a Caribbean cruise.

Two years after Joe's death, she became very ill with bronchial pneumonia. She was forced to stay home, and it was then that she was faced with the emotions that she had not yet dealt with. She cried at times when she did not want to cry. She was faced with grief and loneliness. She experienced frequent episodes of anger and depression. Many nights she agonized in prayer and cried in order to relieve her symptoms of intense grief.

The Lord showed her that she needed to stop and deal with her grief. She needed to feel her pain in order to move through it. The Lord promised her that He would be near and help her.

Betty coped by talking to others about her feelings. She found comfort in prayer, meditation, and studying God's word.

The scriptures that encouraged her were: 'The effectual fervent prayer of a righteous man availeth much' (James 5:16) and 'Fear not . . . for thy Maker is thine husband; the LORD of hosts *is* his name . . . For a small moment have I forsaken thee; but with great mercies will I gather thee . . . but with everlasting kindness will I have mercy on thee, saith the LORD thy Redeemer. O thou afflicted, tossed with tempest, and not comforted . . .' (Isaiah 54:4–11).

Many of Betty's friends were supportive. They allowed her to tell and re-tell things about Joe, as well as to talk about the painful experience of his death.

Playing the piano for the church was therapeutic as well as painful. It was a reminder of their work together in the church.

Betty's sadness and emptiness were heightened during the holidays and special activities. A song could bring tears to her eyes.

At times, Betty had a sense of Joe's presence. Sometimes she looked for him to walk through the door at his usual time.

By acknowledging her loss, feeling her pain and adjusting to her new life style, Betty began to feel a healing in her life. Her job as a nurse was stimulating as well as challenging.

Before Joe's death, their three daughters had been expecting babies. Now Betty enjoys her new grandchildren. She will always miss Joe, but her life changed and she adapted to a new lifestyle.

Normal Reactions to Loss or Crisis

My heart is smitten, and withered like grass;
so that I forget to eat my bread.

Psalm 102:4

*A*cute grief affects the body, mind and spirit. Many normal reactions include:

- A feeling of tightness in your throat.
- A feeling of tightness in your chest or an inability to catch your breath.
- An empty feeling in the stomach.
- A lack of energy.
- A feeling of guilt or anger over things that happened or didn't happen in the relationship.

- A need to tell, re-tell, and remember things about the loved one, particularly in the event of death.
- Crying at unexpected times.

God is ever-present to them that call upon Him. 'God is our refuge and strength, a very present help in trouble' (Psalm 46: 1).

Mary's Story

I am troubled; I am bowed down greatly; I
go mourning all the day long.

Psalm 38:6

*B*rian was an active four-year-old boy; his
parents were just getting used to the diagnosis,
'attention deficit disorder'. He thought that he
was fast enough to outrun a truck: 'Oh Mom,
I'm faster than a truck. I'll be able to get out of its
way.' Shortly after that, his parents found him
dead in their backyard pool.

At first Mary coped fairly well, or so she
thought. Her friends thought that she was doing 'too well'. She was numb with shock, and

then denial, for a couple of years. As life seemed to unfold itself for Mary, her losses multiplied, but none were as bad as the loss of her son. But because that loss was unresolved for her, the losses that followed only complicated her grief.

One day as her daughter Sara was swimming in the community pool, Mary lost sight of her. Mary felt like her heart stood still. Her fear intensified. She began to sweat, and her heart began to pound in her chest. She could hear each heartbeat in her ears. Each beat sounded like a roar. She felt as if she might faint. Suddenly Sara's head came out of the water, and she looked around for her mother. After glancing at her mother, she turned around and swam off.

Mary felt a sense of relief, but could not seem to calm herself. Her head started to pound and ache. Her shoulders and neck felt incredibly tense.

The Physiological Reactions to Distress

My soul is also sore vexed.

Psalm 6:3

Have you ever wondered why you feel anxious, overwhelmed or have an increase in blood pressure and heart rate when you are faced with grief, stress, or crisis? Your body attempts to respond to the stressor in your life. All stressors that you encounter cause you to attempt to adapt to maintain your equilibrium. In attempting to cope, adapt or respond to the stress, the process requires energy.

> And being in an agony . . . his sweat was as it were great drops of blood falling down to the ground.
>
> Luke 22:44

Stressors are internal or external stimuli that cause stress. They produce certain transient biological or psychosocial reactions that may or may not cumulatively lead to certain health consequences. Grief leads to changes in the endocrine, immune, autonomic nervous and cardiovascular systems.

Stress is any situation in which a non-specific demand requires you to respond or take action. In attempting to adapt to maintain your equilibrium, your endocrine and autonomic nervous system respond to adapt to the challenge.

Distress is either harmful, damaging or unpleasant stress.

Adaptation is the capacity of your body to respond in an active way to stressors in a constantly changing environment. The response may be physiological, psychological, motor or cognitive.

The process of adaptation consists of three phases:

1. The alarm reaction.
2. The resistance phase.
3. The exhaustion phase.

This process is called the General Adaptation Syndrome (Seyle 1975).

General Adaptation Syndrome (G.A.S.)

1. THE ALARM REACTION

   With the first response to stress, the body prepares to fight or escape. The autonomic nervous system is stimulated. The following are increased:

   - Blood pressure
   - Heart rate
   - Respiratory rate

   The blood sugar level is raised to make more glucose available to meet the need for increased energy. Mental alertness is

increased. The pituitary gland is stimulated to release hormones from targeted
glands such as the thyroid and adrenals.
The following are increased:

- metabolic rate
- blood volume
- blood glucose
- muscle contractions

Physiological reactions related to release
of epinephrine which occurs during the
alarm reaction include:

- sighing respiration
- shortness of breath
- substernal tightness
- palpitations
- weakness
- crying
- rapid pulse
- sweaty palms
- tensing muscles

2. THE RESISTANCE PHASE

During this stage, the reactions that occurred during the alarm stage have subsided. Your body then attempts to restore and rebuild the defenses used during the alarm stage. Your body adapts to the stressor and begins to resist. Your energy and physical resources attempt to deal with ongoing stressors. The length of the resistant period depends on your body's adaptability as well as the stressor.

During the period of resistance, the hormone cortisone is increased. It is beneficial in helping your body regain homeostasis or a balanced equilibrium. During this stage your emotional and physical resources are being consumed by your efforts to control the stress.

Physiological and emotional signs and symptoms during the resistant stage consist of:

- difficulty in concentrating
- irritability

- frequent anger
- excessive worry or anxiety
- disrupted digestion and elimination

During this time, ulcers or other psycho-physiological disorders may first appear. If stress or unresolved grief is intense or prolonged, the effects of cortisone become potentially harmful and lead to illness, disease, or death.

If a new severe stress arises during the stage of resistance, you can no longer maintain resistance to the stressor and will often enter the exhaustion phase immediately.

3. STAGE OF EXHAUSTION

If stress is severe enough or if the body's supply of energy or ability to use energy is inadequate, you have entered the exhaustion stage. Your defense system and resistance, i.e. your immune system, is lowered, and you become vulnerable to disease and tissue damage. There is an increased susceptibility to stress-induced diseases or illnesses, such as diabetes, skin disorders, stomach ulcers, high blood pressure, asthma, and cancer.

During the exhaustion stage, you no longer maintain resistance to the stressor, and bodily resources become highly taxed as the symptoms of alarm reaction reappear. In extreme cases, resistance collapses and causes death.

Summary

People who have the most emotional distress reactions have the most significant endocrine reaction. Agitated activity and screaming are congruent behaviors associated with the alarm response to extreme distress, crisis, grief or loss. Rage and fear affect biological functions such as blood flow and cardiac rate by increasing the activity in widely distributed nerve fibers in the autonomic nervous system.

Your major task in life is to adapt to change. The response to change and loss (G.A.S.) requires energy. During the resistance stage, even a weak stressor can provoke a strong response in the individual. If a new severe stress arises during the stage of resistance, your immune system will be lowered, and you will enter the exhaustion phase immediately.

Stages of Grief

I am poured out like water, and all my bones
are out of joint; my heart is like wax; it is
melted in the midst of my bowels.

Psalm 22:14

1. Denial/Shock

Denial is a defense mechanism that you
use when something is so painful that it
threatens the mind. The mind refuses to
acknowledge a thought, feeling, or reality. Denial acts as protection from the full
impact of the loss. It is a functional coping mechanism, allowing you to get tasks
completed.

Shock is a sudden and violent distur-
bance of the mind or emotion. Any reaction to bad news is normal and okay. You
may feel hysterical or icy calm. It is best
to be gentle with yourself and let reactions happen.

> The LORD is nigh unto them that are
> of a broken heart.
>
> Psalm 34:18

2. Anger/Guilt

Anger is part of the normal reaction to
loss. It is a basic response to extreme dis-
pleasure or exasperation. Anger is characterized by irritability, bitterness, and an
impulse to strike out at an object or person. Anger can be a functional coping
mechanism, if it isn't prolonged beyond
two or three weeks. Anger generally increases adrenaline and energy.

Guilt occurs when you turn your anger
inward. It is an emotion that is based on
a combination of anxiety and regret or
sadness.

3. Bargaining

Bargaining is generally the briefest stage of grief. It is an attempt to gain time through making promises to a higher power ('Let me live to see my children grown, God, and I will be exemplary in my life') or to one's self ('If I survive this, I will certainly take better care of myself'). It is a time to think about any unfinished business and complete or come to terms with it.

4. Depression/Despair

The Complete Guide to Your Emotions & Your Health states that depression can be defined and experienced as internalized anger. It is reactive in nature and is past oriented. The past is unfinished and still affects the present. Depression is a normal part of the grief-growth process and is characterized by a sense of worthlessness and the absence of emotional, physical, or mental energy. Physical energy is so low that you may experience difficulty in concentrating and thinking clearly.

Recovery will occur when you have worked through repressed emotions or have a renewed interest in living. This process generally takes from a few weeks to a few months.

Despair is defined as the feeling of hopelessness. It is also reactive in nature, and one's mood seems low. When a person despairs, the future seems dark, pointless and without meaning. Hope is abandoned. By restoring hope of a future worth living, despair disappears.

5. Acceptance

Acceptance is the final phase in the grief cycle. You *are* able to accept the loss. This is not the same as resignation. Acceptance gives you a sense of peace, and you are able to move on to the emotions of renewed life. The main characteristic of acceptance is that once again you are able to enjoy life and to experience pleasure in living without guilt, anger, or depression. You can look to the future, not to the past.

Summary

Perhaps it is not so important whether you win or lose, but it's how you play the game called LIFE. Many times you will lose. Loss occurs during every life cycle. Frequently you cannot control circumstances, but you can accept responsibility for yourself. Knowing and understanding the phases and tasks of grieving can help you, not only to work out your own grief and loss, but to help others do the same.

Experiencing grief after loss is necessary, and the grieving process must be completed before your health can be restored. The only way out of grief is to go through it. The greater the loss, the more you will experience the stages of denial, shock, anger, guilt, bargaining, depression, despair, and acceptance.

Tasks of Grieving

To everything there is a season, and a time
to every purpose under the heaven . . . a
time to heal . . . a time to weep, and a time
to laugh; a time to mourn . . .

Ecclesiastes 3:1,3,4

1. Make it real

Shock and denial are normal, but after
one or two weeks, you must accept your
loss. Probably the easiest loss to believe is
death. Divorce or loss of a job have no
accompanying rituals.

Our society follows certain rituals when death occurs. Being present at the death, seeing the body, or attending the funeral or memorial service can help you accept the reality of the loss.

Because rituals facilitate grief, it is more difficult to come to terms with these losses and to obtain closure, which you must accomplish. Without the ritual event you can too easily avoid your pain and carry your sorrow within you for years. By planning the ritual, you will have a time to deal directly with your loss and pain. A ritual or memorial is a way to remember, and sharing memories is a way to say goodbye to your loss.

Just as you go through a graduation ceremony after completing college to indicate completion or closure, you can plan a memorial service to close the grieving process. Even in divorce you can plan a celebration to remember the good times that you shared together.

2. Feel the pain

Sorrow is a reaction, a painful longing for the mourner's lost relationship. It is characterized by sharp emotional pain, weeping, sobbing, and even moaning. To process your grief, you must feel the pain, which may include such physical manifestations as shortness of breath, a feeling of tightness in your chest, fatigue, and an inability to sleep, even though you feel tired. You may even have a feeling of temporary insanity.

3. Adjust to the loss

During this part of the grieving process, you feel a sense of peace regarding your loss. You can look to the future with new hope and not be so preoccupied with the past. You will still continue to experience occasional waves of emotional pain and sadness over your loss, but the frequency and intensity of the pain will be less. The wound is still present, but it is almost healed.

Renewal of life offers you the opportunity to find new meaning in life. Your responsibilities, obligations, and emotional support system will probably change.

If you have lost a mate, whether through death or divorce, your self-identity will change. Your role changes from being a part of a couple to being single.

Summary

The grief process cannot be suppressed or resolved with drugs. Medications may help with short-term relief, but the grief process is prolonged if you use medications to escape the emotional pain. You must experience emotional pain. The process of grief cannot be rushed.

To lose a spouse is to suffer one of life's most profound losses, and to lose a child is to change your life forever. Parental grief is more severe than other types of bereavement—more intense, more complex, and longer lasting.

To move through the journey of grief, you must complete three tasks:

1. Make it real
2. Feel the pain
3. Adjust to the loss

Weeping may endure for a night, but joy *cometh* in the morning.

Psalm 30:5

Grief Recovery Concepts

Blessed are they that mourn: for they shall be comforted.

Matt. 5:4

1. The way out of grief is through it.
2. The very worst grief is yours.
3. Grief is hard work.
4. Effective grief work is not done alone.

Amy's Story

> . . . the king was much moved and went up
> to the chamber . . . and wept: thus he said,
> 'O my son, my son, my son! Would God I
> had died for thee.'
>
> 2 Samuel 18:33

Full of energy, six-year-old Scott loved to run and play. He played to win. Work was play to Scott. He loved to help his father in his parents' cleaning service.

Scott's approach was gentle. He tended to shyly hold his head down and not make much eye contact with others. He generally had a twinkle in his eyes. Scott knew no strangers. He was a friend to everyone. He was alert to what was going on around him. His siblings, as well as his friends, looked to him for direction; and bravely, often without speaking, he took the lead.

Playing ball with his brother and sister, he kicked the ball and it landed on the roof and stopped. The roof was flat, and the ball would not return to them without some help.

He ran onto the freshly mopped floor, looking for his dad. His mom yelled at him to stay off of the wet floor.

Soon Scott's mom saw the children passing by with a ladder. She told them to wait until their dad had time to help them. She hurriedly pushed the mop bucket back to the janitor's room to clean the mop. She heard the children up on the roof and felt a sense of panic rise within her. She ran out of the building and yelled for the children to come down. As she headed for their van, she heard a thud. Her mind refused to accept what she suspected. Then she saw Scott laying very still on the ground. She felt for his pulse: his eyes were rolled back.

Scott's sister and brother were still on the roof, crying hysterically. Scott's mother, Amy, reached for her two and a half year old son: he was trying to climb up the ladder. Steve, their father, scooped up Scott and placed him into the van. Amy's mind was racing, and she felt alarmed: maybe they weren't supposed to move Scott! Steve's mind was clouded with confusion. He didn't know what he should do next. Amy told him to call 9-1-1. She then, by herself, put the ladder away. She called her mom, and then their pastor.

Amy's parents arrived on the scene, followed by the pastor and his wife. The fire department as well as the ambulance arrived. The ambulance raced Scott away to the hospital, leaving them with the sense of emptiness.

Amy's dad took the other children to the hospital, while her mother rode with them. Amy was able to do the tasks at hand, but her mind was clouded with turmoil and a sense of alarm.

When Amy and Steve arrived at the hospital, the emergency department personnel allowed them only a few minutes with Scott. They touched him and told him that they loved him. Then he was rushed off to the X ray department for tests. He remained unconscious.

The brain specialist told them that Scott's brain was swelling and only time would tell if he would wake up or improve. The neurologist remained neutral with his opinion.

As the family waited and waited, Amy knew by faith that Scott would open his eyes and talk to them. She longed to take him in her arms and tell him she loved him, but the many tubes that connected him to machines intimidated her.

Amy felt a peace that God was in control, whether Scott lived or died. The pastor's wife sat with her while Steve and their pastor did another cleaning job.

Sharing some delightful experiences, Amy was able to laugh. The laughter helped to relieve some of the pent-up tension. She didn't understand how she could be laughing at such a devastating time, which added to her feelings of guilt.

Both Amy and Steve stayed with Scott at the hospital that night. The nurse gave some encouragement: Scott seemed to be minimally responding. Then suddenly his heart rate went up to the two hundreds and his temperature went up to about one hundred and four degrees. To Amy, that was the turning point for Scott. She felt that his condition was worsening. Another CT scan showed no improvement.

The night nurse was supportive, as well as informative. Both Steve and Amy felt a pang of insecurity as she went off duty.

Amy went home to shower, then over to her parents' home to see her other children. During that time, the neurosurgeon called to say that he wanted Scott taken to a particular hospital in San Francisco. He felt that they were better equipped to care for Scott.

Amy was going to fly down to San Francisco alone, but the thought of being alone terrorized her. Steve went with her. Their pastor and his wife took them to the airport. They were early, so they went into the restaurant. Eating did not come easy. Amy took a precious promises Bible from her purse. She read from Rev. 21:4:

And God shall wipe away all tears from their
eyes and there shall be no more death, neither sorrow, nor crying, neither shall there
be any more pain: for the former things are
passed away.

From that moment, this verse became her favorite, which she continues to cling to.

Amy and Steve boarded the airplane, which
began their journey of sorrow. To my understanding, they were still in a state of denial,
shock, of the inevitable. Sorrow is "pain or affliction of the mind from loss or disappoint-
ment." It is true that they felt sad with what had
happened when Scott fell, but too numb to
grieve.

As the plane began to descend, they went
straight down into a blanket of clouds, which
added to their tension. They arrived at the huge
airport and had to take a shuttle to the main building. There they had to take another shuttle to
the hospital.

The process of getting to Scott's location in
the hospital was cumbersome. The surroundings

were unknown territory to them, which added to their confusion. They arrived at the hospital, then asked at the information desk where they could find Scott. They were instructed to go to the sixth floor; then they were directed to use the phone. No one was there to meet them or to lead them. They were told to wait in the waiting room.

After waiting, which seemed like a very long time, they asked for assistance from a lady walking by. At last, the doctor came and led them to where Scott lay. The name of the nurse caring for Scott was Sandy; the same name as one of Amy's sisters. That gave them both a slight feeling of familiarity in this cold and unfamiliar process. Sandy was kind and offered them comfort.

Amy and Steve had brought Scott's bunny, B.J., which they put in bed with him. They touched Scott and told him they loved him. Again Amy wanted to take him in her arms and hold him close, but the tubes were overwhelming and frightening. The nurse did explain what some of the tubes and monitors meant, but their minds could not seem to accept any technical information.

Steve called his family in Canada. While discussing plans for them to come to San Francisco, the nurse spoke up and told him to not make any plans until they had talked to the doctor.

Until that moment, they felt they had a sense of hope from the nurse, but now time seemed to come to a sudden halt to them. Amy began to suspect what they already feared.

They waited for the pastor and his wife to arrive. They called Amy's parents, but there was no answer. They called the number of their pastor's home in Eureka, but again no one was home. They felt totally alone and helpless.

They later found out that Amy's parents were driving down with their other children. In the meantime, the nurse took Amy's hand and told her that the doctor wanted to talk to them. There were too many people around; Amy and Steve felt overwhelmed—like they were suffocating. The air was heavy. Their minds were spinning, not daring to imagine the worst.

The nurse tried to comfort Amy. Her small hints, in trying to prepare them for what was coming only brought irritation. Amy felt many emotions surface, including anger, fear, and despair. She trusted no one. Then the news came crashing down on them. Scott was dead. One of the doctors began to explain that they had done numerous tests on Scott, and he did not respond to any of them. They pronounced him brain dead.

It was difficult for Amy and Steve to stay focused. Everything was going much too fast. What was being said made no sense at all. Scott was alive! He looked at peace, and his skin color looked good. They were lying. They couldn't possibly know what they were talking about.

Amy felt cold shock waves run through her blood. She didn't cry. She felt frozen. She felt angry. Then they were asked a difficult question. 'Would Amy and Steve consider organ donation?'

Immediately Amy said, 'No!' At that moment, Amy felt the sole purpose of the doctors in sending Scott to San Francisco was to take his 'parts'.

Steve was so mad that he felt that they had compared Scott to a scrap car. 'Now he's dead, so take his parts.' They were told that they didn't need to make a decision right away. Steve got up to call his family. As he got up, he apologized for the way he felt. Amy told him that he did not need to apologize.

The pastor and his wife from the San Francisco church arrived and met them in Scott's room. They were emotionally supportive, and brought much comfort. Amy and Steve talked about organ donation with their pastor. He told them that it was their decision whether or not to consent to donation.

Amy thought about Scott's beautiful big eyes. They were so full of life. She felt that she didn't want anyone else to see out of his sparkling, dark blue eyes. They did consent to organ donation, but not eye donation. After signing the consent form, they just wanted everything to be over.

Amy's parents got to the hospital. She told her father that Scott was dead. In shock, he refused to believe what she was saying. He told her that they had just seen Scott, and he looked good. She explained that the machines were keeping him alive, but Scott was brain dead.

Steve and Amy met with their two older children, Jennifer (nine) and Jeff (six). Cody (two) was riding a bike in the hallway. Amy sat Jennifer on one knee and Jeff on the other knee. They told them that Scott had died. They all wept together. They asked many questions. They did want to see Scott, which was the last time they saw him look 'alive'. They said their goodbyes.

They continued to experience many intense emotions and fears. 'What if he really is still alive, and they take his organs?' Amy knew deep in her soul that Jesus could still raise Scott up. They went to their motel. Steve could not be consoled. Nothing brought him comfort. Nothing eased his pain. Even though no one blamed him, he blamed himself for allowing the children to get up on the roof.

At times after Scott's death, Jeff was angry and insinuated that Scott had jumped or died on purpose. Jeff asked his mother if Scott could jump down from heaven.

At times, Jennifer would sit down and cry. She felt bad for the times she had been mean to her brother.

Jeff kept thinking about his brother, and sometimes he would cry when no one was watching.

Seven to eight months after Scott's death, Amy felt like her grief was ten-fold to what it was when he actually died. Her waves of emotional pain come in like a great flood. At times, it took very little to trigger her emotions.

Often Steve feels great sadness from the loss of his son. He is silent with his pain.

At times, Amy and Steve appreciate the moments that they can be distracted from their grief. They are able to find pleasure in doing things together, including white-water rafting.

A Child's Reaction to Grief

I did mourn as a dove: mine eyes fail *with looking* upward: O Lord, I am oppressed; undertake for me.

Isaiah 38:14

A child's response to loss is different from that of an adult. The reaction to loss is age dependent.

To understand how a child responds to loss and how your child can effectively move through his grief, you must first understand the stages of cognitive and psychosocial development.

To a child, hearing the one he/she is close to is dead, doesn't necessarily bring a response. It's the 'missing them' or the 'goneness' that the child responds to.

Because children are concrete in their thinking, it is best to use words like 'death' or 'dead'. Do not say that the loved one 'passed away', 'went to heaven', or 'is sleeping'. Answer his questions as simply as possible.

Adult's Reaction to Grief	Child's Reaction to Grief
Shock and denial	Shock and denial
Anger	Act out anger
Bargaining	Magical thinking; bargaining
Depression	Sadness, rage, or withdrawal
Resolution and acceptance	Resolution and acceptance

Children have the capacity to heal, but they cannot heal until their parents or significant caregiver begins to heal.

From the time of birth through old age, or death, (whichever comes first), you move through different developmental stages. Each development stage brings different reactions and understanding to loss. As a child passes through each cognitive and psychosocial stage, he must reprocess his grief, to understand the loss.

- Cognitive refers to the mental process of comprehension, judgment, memory, and reasoning.
- Cognitive development is an individual's ability to mentally process information.
- Developmental tasks are age-specific achievements identified by Erickson.

Taylor (1994)

These cognitive/psychosocial stages include the following:

Age	Piagetian Cognitive Stage of Development	Eriksonian Stages of Psychosocial Development	Reactions to Loss	Child's Concept of Death	Helpful Approaches
Birth to age 2	Sensorimotor stage: Views life through his senses: touch, smell, taste, sight, hearing: Views, perceives that significant others or things come and go: i.e., parents, family; Peek-a-Boo. Learns through senses and movement.	Basic trust vs mistrust: Attach to significant person–trust develops when loved one is again present.	General distress. Cries, fitful sleep.	No concept of death, but reacts to loss.	Consistent nurturing person.

Age	Piagetion Cognitive Stage of Development	Eriksonian Stages of Psychosocial Development	Reactions to Loss	Child's Concept of Death	Helpful Approaches
2–7	Preoperational stage: Cannot reason beyond what they see, hear or experience.	(1°–3) Autonomy vs shame: Sense of dependence and self-control (3–5°) Initiative vs guilt: Ability to initiate activities and see them through.	(2–5) Confusion, fear, nightmares: Understands profound event has occurred. May seem unaffected by loss. May react to others' emotions.	Death is temporary and reversible Death is seen as a departure or separation.	Reassurance. Secure loving environment. Drawing. Funeral ritual. Play.

Age	Piagetion Cognitive Stage of Development	Eriksonian Stages of Psychosocial Development	Reactions to Loss	Child's Concept of Death	Helpful Approaches
		(5) Compare their abilities with other children.	Understanding of death or loss is limited.	(5–8) Wants to understand death in concrete manner: Denial, anger, fear, sadness. Thinks it won't happen to them.	

Age	Piagetian Cognitive Stage of Development	Eriksonian Stages of Psychosocial Development	Reactions to Loss	Child's Concept of Death	Helpful Approaches
7–11	Period of formal operations: Thought becomes logical. Can consider points of view, other than own.	(5°–12) Industry vs inferiority: Successful teaching of self against peers leads to feelings of industry.	(5–8): General distress and confusion: necessarily May act as if nothing happened. (8-12): May want to conform with peers.	Death is irreversible but not inevitable. Death may be personified and viewed as destructive.	Simple honesty. Answers questions simply. Dead is dead. Physical outlets. Funeral ritual.

Age	Piagetion Cognitive Stage of Development	Eriksonian Stages of Psychosocial Development	Reactions to Loss	Child's Concept of Death	Helpful Approaches
			Facade of coping: 'it's okay' when it's not okay. Finality of death understood. Phobic behaviours. Morbid curiosity.	Explanations for death are naturalistic and physiological.	Play, color, draw, reading, sculpting. Reassurance about future. Talk about feelings. Write.

Age	Piagetion Cognitive Stage of Development	Eriksonian Stages of Psychosocial Development	Reactions to Loss	Child's Concept of Death	Helpful Approaches
12–15	Period of formal operations: Characterized by adaptability and flexibility.	(Adolescent) Identity vs role confusion.	Shock, anxiety distress, anger depression, despair. Less coping mechanisms than adult.	Death is irreversible, universal and inevitable. Death is still seen as a personal but distant event. Explanations for death are physiological and theological.	Discuss feelings. Peer support groups. Consistent environment. Involvement in family.

How You Can Live With Loss

And he took them, and went aside privately
into a desert place . . .

Luke 9:10

*Y*ou can help yourself move toward recovery by taking care of:

A. Emotional Needs

1. FIND A WAY TO EXPRESS YOUR FEEL-
    INGS

    If you have problems verbalising your
    feelings, there are many non-verbal ac-
    tivities that can help you to express your

grief. Writing or talking about your feelings helps you face what confuses or scares you. By naming or describing your feelings or pain, the healing process goes into action. It gives simplicity to your feelings, values, and priorities. Journal keeping allows you to be honest with yourself.

2. ASK FOR HELP

Symptom Control makes the claim that approximately one of every three persons who suffers a major loss may require special help. Don't hesitate to ask for help or state your need, particularly to those who offer their help or support. Be specific with your requests: say that you want someone to go out to lunch with you or to drive you to the cemetery. If you want a shoulder to cry on, say that.

3. ACCEPT HELP

You may need help during critical periods like holidays, birthdays, anniversaries, weddings, and so on. Talk about your loved one at your holiday gatherings. Lighting a candle, either at a holiday gathering, or alone, can be a way of acknowledging your memory of your loved one. Choose whomever you would like to be with on those special dates. Don't assume that the best people to spend the day with are the ones you generally see every day. Someone who has also suffered a major loss might be a more comfortable person for you to be with during your critical time. Sometimes going to a special place you enjoy is helpful. Be good to yourself on these special days.

4. BE KIND TO YOURSELF

Expect to experience waves of sadness. The intensity of grief gradually lessens. A favorite song, seeing a couple enjoying one another's company, or any reminder that brings the reality of your loss into focus will probably cause you emotional pain. Keep yourself rested and don't knowingly put yourself in difficult situations. Allow your feelings to surface;

express and honor them. Cry when you need to and laugh when you want to. Laughing and crying both provide release from the tension that you may be experiencing.

B. Physical Needs

1. KEEP YOURSELF HEALTHY

Nutrition and physical well-being are vital resources in grief recovery. Eat on a regular schedule, whether you want to or not. Eating small, frequent meals helps control your blood sugar, energy level, and weight.

Physical activity improves your general attitude and health. Sustained exercise can help control some symptoms as well as emotional reactions to grief. Exercise itself has a calming effect. Aerobic exercise is shown to reduce depression and stress (due to the release of endorphins). Gentle exercise also helps relieve pent-up feelings and the stress of grief.

Massage is therapeutic because it opens channels of energy. It dilates blood vessels, promotes circulation, cleanses the body of toxins by promoting the flow of lymph, and relieves muscle tension.

2. GET PLENTY OF REST

Working through grief is tiring and can wear you out. Adequate rest is important to help you get through the tasks that need to be accomplished, as well as allowing you to do the things that you enjoy doing. Usually, physical relaxation is the state in which the body can best begin to heal itself.

3. BE ALERT TO PROBLEMS

Medical problems such as shortness of breath, dizziness, headaches, nausea, gastrointestinal distress, and fatigue may be stress related. If they persist, call your physician.

C. Social Needs

MAKE TIME FOR FUN

Schedule time for both work and play. Play is just as important to your well-being as work. A break from your daily activities helps you to relax and have fun.

Look for things to make you laugh. Set goals and work to reach them. Goals give you a purpose and direction in how to live. Start with short-term goals. List what you'd like to accomplish. You might begin with activities such as letter writing, visiting with friends, or preparing a favorite meal. Set time limits for completing your goals.

D. Spiritual Needs

For each accomplishment and adversity in life there is an accompanying spiritual dimension—an opportunity to discover deeper meaning and to affirm the profound existence of a higher power. What are your stronger and more important beliefs? Is there anything that you can count on to support your feelings of security, or can you trust that all will work out for the best? Where do you find joy, satisfaction, and fulfilment?

Hope is necessary for life. There is nothing more essential to life than hope. Hope brings meaning and purpose to one's existence.

Happiness, too, is important. You can grieve and still experience a sense of happiness and peace.

What is the key to happiness? Forgiveness. It is the key to peace of mind. You may need to forgive yourself or the one who has left you. You may feel angry at the deceased loved one for leaving you. Maybe you are left with children to raise. Or perhaps you feel angry, because now that the children are grown, you have the time and money to do the things that you were not able to do while raising your family.

The ability to feel peace and happiness lies within each one of us. Forgiveness is a decision. To be forgiven, you must forgive. 'For if we forgive men their trespasses, your heavenly Father will also forgive you' (Matthew 6:14).

Forgiveness is a journey of the heart. It goes much deeper than words. It is an act of letting go of anger or any thought of judgment. Now is a good time to soul search and assess your own feelings and attitude. Be kind and gentle to yourself. Be patient, and feel peace flood your soul as you let go of the hurts from your past.

Forgive for the sake of your own wellness. Forgiveness allows you to take control of your own heart and life. It is something that you do for yourself. You will set your heart in a new direction away from the past and pain—toward the present and peace. Live as though you have been healed. Envision yourself without the burden of unforgiveness. Practice or pretend that the restraint from freedom is not there, and feel the load lifted. Then take steps to enhance the healing process. Think about what you would like to re- solve and what it is that you would like to have different in your life. You may desire to make amends with an old friend or relative. Or perhaps there is something that you wish you had said to your de- ceased loved one. You could write a let- ter to your loved one, explaining how you feel, and then destroy the letter.

It was Christmas time two years after my husband, Danny, had left me. I was down on my knees praying. I asked the Lord if there was anything between us (the Lord and I) that blocked our communication. The Lord said to me, 'Vickee, you need to forgive Danny.' I immediately said, 'But Lord, I deserve to own these feelings that I have!' I felt as if I could not get a prayer through, and I finally said, 'Okay, Lord, if you help me and show me how to for- give him, I will.'

The rest seemed easy as I submitted my feelings to the Lord. 'Submit yourselves therefore to God' (James 4:7). The peace that I felt in my heart was a real surprise! It felt as if a heavy load was lifted off my shoulders, and I felt as if I was released from bondage. I hadn't even realized that I had bitterness or an unforgiving spirit towards Danny.

And be ye kind one to another, tender-hearted, forgiving one another, even as God for Christ's sake hath forgiven you.

Ephesians 4:32

Summary

Art Linkletter said, 'Life turns out best for those who make the best of the way life turns out' (Allen, 1980).

During crisis, adversity, or accomplishment, the spiritual realm can be your most important stabilizing force. The journey through healing can promote spiritual growth.

Find activities that give you pleasure and that are good for your mental and physical well-being. Focus on enjoyment, relaxation and health. Fun helps shift your perspective, increases your flexibility, raises your energy level, boosts your desire to live, and helps you to plan for the future. Hope enables the living to continue to live and dying to die with a sense of peace or meaning to one's life.

A merry heart doeth good like a medicine:
but a broken spirit drieth the bones.
Proverbs 17:22

Forgiveness frees you from bondage, and brings healing to your spirit. To forgive and to ask forgiveness is a decision—your decision.

Unfinished Business

Search me, O God, and know my heart: try
me and know my thoughts: And see if there
be any wicked way in me, and lead me in
the way everlasting.

Psalm 139:23–24

*U*nfinished business, something that is incomplete in your life, robs you of a sense of peace.
When you are faced with a major loss, your
awareness of any unfinished business in your
relationships with others becomes apparent. Iden-
tifying the feelings that come up when something
is incomplete in your life can help you to process your feelings and complete what is important to you in your relationships.

Are you willing to let go of the sorrows and hurts of your past? Or do you feel you deserve to own those feelings of sadness and resentment? Unforgiveness binds you to your past and blocks happiness in the present moment.

To live during the most significant times in your life is to live in the moment. To live in the moment is the biggest gift that you can give yourself. As you read this book you may say, 'But the most enjoyable time in my life has passed. My loved one is dead, or has divorced me, and my heart no longer knows happiness.' Your suffering or affliction can bring renewal. You have the chance to plan new goals and to evaluate your purpose in life.

In order to live in the present moment, you must attend to today's pleasures, joys, and burdens. You need to release your old hurts and guilt, whether those feelings are real or perceived. Once you no longer have those festering wounds to blame for your present trouble and sorrow, you will have the freedom to control your own life.

To identify unfinished business in your life, ask yourself the following questions:

- Am I absorbed with the thought of a person or a past experience?
- If I knew that I was terminally ill and could make one telephone call, who would I call? What would I say? (This gets you in touch with what's not being said.) What is keeping you from making that call?

How to Complete Unfinished Business

. . . this one thing I do, forgetting those things
which are behind, and reaching forth unto
those things which are before . . .

Philippians 3:13

Talk about it, write about it, and let go of
the past. The more definitely and completely you
move the pain outside yourself, the cleaner your
wound will heal.

Writing or talking about your pain or feelings brings clarity to whatever is bothering you.
The healing process is in action, also, when you
distinctly clarify your values, and work toward
the solutions that you desire.

As a scar strengthens a wound, so does writing or talking heal your pain. There may always be a scar resulting from your painful experience, but once you work through your hurts and subsequent healing has taken place, the mark can prove to yourself and to others that you did survive the difficult times.

Identify your emotions: 'I feel cheated, angry, mad, betrayed, abandoned, lonely,' etc. Be honest with your feelings. The scripture, 'And ye shall know the truth, and the truth shall make you free' (John 8:32), refers to the passage of spiritual freedom. But being truthful also provides the gateway to emotional freedom.

Summary

To have a sense of peace you must resolve any unfinished business. This may simply mean finding closure in a relationship. Healing the pain of the past takes time. Painful memories may cause a temporary ache in your heart, just as old wounds can ache, if bumped. Those who matter to you can still inflict pain, but it is your choice as to how much you are affected by that pain.

Conclusion

Peace I leave with you, my peace I give unto you: not as the world giveth, give I unto you. Let not your heart be troubled, neither let it be afraid.

John 14:27

References

Bates, M. and Keirsey, D., *Please Understand Me*, Delmar: Prometheus Nemesis Book Company, (1984).

Collins, G., *How To Be A People Helper*, Ventura: Regal Books (1975).

Covey, S.R., *The 7 Habits of Highly Effective People*, New York: Fireside (1989).

Darley, G.M., Glucksberg, S. and Kinchla, R. A., *Psychology*, Fifth Edition, New Jersey: Prentice Hall (1991).

Deits, B., *Life After Loss*, Tucson: Fisher Books (1988).

Hemfelt, R. and Warren, P., Kids Who Carry Our Pain, Nashville: Thomas Nelson, Inc. (1990).

Kaye, P., *Symptom Control*, Essex: Hospice Education Institute, Inc. (1989).

Padus, E., *The Complete Guide To Your Emotions & Your Health*, Philadelphia: Rodale Press, Inc. (1986).

Perry, A.G., and Potter, P.A., *Fundamentals of Nursing*, St. Louis: Mosby Year Book (1993).

Seyle, H., *Stress Without Distress*, New York: Harper & Row Publishers, Inc. (1975).

Stevens, V.D., *Grief Work*, Nashville: Broadman Press (1990).

To order additional copies of

Have your credit card ready and call:

1-877-421-READ (7323)

or please visit our web site at
www.pleasantword.com

Also available at: www.amazon.com

Printed in the United States
220799BV00001B/11/A

9 781579 215804